The Gypsy and the Poet

DAVID MORLEY is partly Romani and sometimes writes in Romani dialect. His poetry has won numerous awards and prizes. An ecologist and naturalist by background, David is also known for his pioneering ecological poetry installations within natural landscapes and the creation of 'slow poetry' sculptures and I-Cast poetry films. He writes essays, criticism and reviews for the *Guardian* and *Poetry Review*. A leading international advocate of creative writing both inside and outside the academy, David is the author of *The Cambridge Introduction to Creative Writing* (2007) and co-editor of *The Cambridge Companion to Creative Writing* (2012). He currently teaches at the University of Warwick where he is Professor of Writing.

D1454647

DAVID MORLEY

The Gypsy and the Poet

CARCANET

First published in Great Britain in 2013 by
Carcanet Press Limited
Alliance House
Cross Street
Manchester M2 7AQ

www.carcanet.co.uk

A CIP catalogue record for this book is available from the British Library

ISBN 978 1 84777 124 7

The publisher acknowledges financial assistance from Arts Council England

Typeset by XL Publishing Services, Exmouth
Printed and bound in England by SRP Ltd, Exeter

I hid my love when young till I
Couldn't bear the buzzing of a fly;
I hid my love to my despite
Till I could not bear to look at light:
I dare not gaze upon her face
But left her memory in each place;
Where'er I saw a wild flower lie
I kissed and bade my love goodbye.

John Clare

Acknowledgements

Thanks are due to the following publications in which some of these poems first appeared: *English*; *Fingerdance*; *Gists and Piths*; *The Guardian*; *Horizon Review*; *The John Clare Society Journal*; *Magma*; *Modern Poetry in Translation*; *Poetry Review*; *The Rialto*; *Salt*; *Stand*; *The Wolf*; and the anthology *Best British Poetry 2012*, edited by Sasha Dugdale (Salt Publications, 2012). Some of the poems have also been featured on the blog *And Other Poems*, and the radio programmes *Late Night Live* (ABC, Australia) and *The Verb* (BBC Radio 3). The 'bard boxes' (see notes) featured in the RSPB magazine *Birds*. Some poems were part of a Slow Art Trail commissioned by Chrysalis Arts sited within Strid Wood in Bolton Abbey, and were released as poetry films on I-TunesU and YouTube. A number of poems were part of an online chapbook *On Not Rushing at Waterfalls*, released by Silkworms Ink. Some poems appeared in the limited edition pamphlet *The Night of the Day* from Nine Arches Press. The author thanks all true friends and first readers, especially Siobhan Keenan, Peter Blegvad, Jonathan Bate, the Romany Theatre Company, and past and present editors at Carcanet, Judith Willson and Helen Tookey.

Contents

The Poet

The Invisible Gift

John Clare weaves English words into a nest
and in the cup he stipples rhyme, like mud,
to clutch the shape of something he can hold
but not yet hear; and in the hollow of his hearing,
he feathers a space with a down of verbs
and nouns heads-up. There. Clare lays it down
and nestles over its forming sound: taps and lilts,
the steady knocking of the nib on his hand until
it hatches softly beneath him. And when he peers
below his palm, he spies its eyes, hears its peeps,
but does not know yet what to think. He strokes
its tottering yolk-wet crown; feels a nip against
his thumb, buds of muscle springy at the wing, and all
the hungers of the world to come for this small singing.

THE GYPSY

Finished planting my ariculas – went a
botanising after ferns and orchises and caught a
cold in the wet grass which has made me as bad
as ever – got the tune of 'highland Mary' from
Wisdom Smith a gipsey and pricked another
sweet tune without name as he fiddled it

John Clare, journal entry

Wisdom Smith Pitches his Bender on Emmonsales Heath, 1819

When yeck's tardrad yeck's beti ten oprey,
kair'd yeck's beti yag anglo the wuddur,
ta nash'd yeck's kekauvi by the kekauviskey saster.

Wisdom leans against an ash tree, shouldering his violin,
slipping the bow to stroke the strings that stay silent
at distance. All John Clare hears is a heron's cranking
and the frozen bog creaking beneath his tread
until that ash tree bows with fieldfares and redwings
and the birds' tunes rise up and twine with Wisdom's.
The men gossip an hour and John Clare writes down
the tune 'Highland Mary' and the Gypsy's given names.
Once Clare is gone the birds refasten to the ash-crown.
Wisdom hacks and stamps the heather beneath his tent,
claps a blanket on springy furze to serve as mattress
and hooks a nodding kettle to the kettle-iron.
He hangs his head, listens, and shoulders the violin.
By practice and by pricking to mind he will master this.

The Ditch

I usd to drop down behind a hedge bush or dyke and write down
my things upon the crown of my hat

As John Clare rises from the ditch where he writes,
frogs bob up through duckweed and roll their eyelids.
The poet's coat and hat, they thought, *were rain-clouds.*
The scribbling pen and riffling paper: they were the rain.
The cloud and rain have moved like lovers out of sight.
Woodlice wake under bark. Nests nudge from within.
Buds are easter-hedged with eggs. A world unwinds
unwinding a world: hedges are easter-egged with buds;
woodlice wake under nests; bark nudges from within;
the lovers and rain move like clouds out of sight;
a scribbling paper and riffling rain: they are the pen;
a thought's hat and coat and rain-cloud: they are poets;
frogs roll up through duckweed and bob their eyelids.
And John Clare settles down by a ditch, where he writes.

John Clare's Notes

Tute has shoon'd the lav pazorrus.
Dovodoy is so is kored gorgikonaes 'Trusted'.

'Pazorrus'. A password. Wisdom Smith taught his nags
in Romani. He made them shine and stamp in brass rigs.
The Gypsy wanted rid of debt full stop. A farmer harrying
him for money for meat bills, well, he couldn't stop smirking
as Wisdom's beasts flounced and flashed. 'This mare for your debt.
That light-tailed foal for forty guineas flat.' The agreement was spat.
Wisdom's horses didn't speak Farmer and came clopping back.
The Gypsy bought them half-price and trotted home in the black:
'Two thousand sleeves as there are tricks. Two thousand
Traveller words holding another card behind the hand.'
Sure as a stallion Wisdom had the triciest part of the trick
and told his daughter Salome who told her granddaughter Lettice
who passed it on to a poet who wrote down a word, 'pazorrus'.
It is what the Gentiles call 'trusted', that is, in their debt.

Magpies

When Gorgio mushe's merripen and Romany Chal's
merripen wells kettaney, kek kost merripen see.

'This atrosious tribe of wandering vagabonds ought
to be made outlaws and exterminated from the earth' –
A Clergyman Writes. John Clare strides to Emmonsales Heath
with the poisonous passage. Wisdom lights his pipe with it.
'Spark one up for yourself, brother, but don't scorch a sonnet
by mistake.' (Clare is scribbling lines on the brim of his hat,
his paper riffling in the breeze.) 'My dad said all along:
when the Gentile way of living and the Gypsy way of living
come together, well, that is anything but a good way of living;
except for riming and your botanising and your good pie, poet...'
Two jabbing magpies strut about the camp on a pin-prick search.
'Take those twin piebald preachers begging for our bread.
They would pick out our eyes and hearts were we lying dead.
All that holds them off is life. The grave is an empty church.'

A Walk

Kekkeno jinava mande ne burreder denne chavo.

John Clare has cider; Wisdom Smith has loaves and cheddar.
They both have good legs. Nine miles of heath and heather
to heaven and nine miles home. By noon they are soaked
and sheltering under one of Wisdom's sprung willow benders.
'You say you want leaving alone to get on with riming,
that you need a house for the task, with British oaks
for a roof and the best of slate on that.' John is writing.
'That light-tailed foal there. See how she lolls in wet grass.
Blue-bottles and horse-flies let her be to roll or doze
she not smelling of fear or love or any such daftnesses.'
But John cannot warm to April squalls under canvas.
He pockets his poem. 'I know no more than a child, John,
but I know what to know and this is home.' Clare bows
to the Gypsy; the Gypsy to Clare. 'Where is my home, Wisdom?'

The Gamekeeper

Kek koskipen si to jal roddring after Romany chals.
When tute came to dick lende nestist to latch yeck o o' lende.

John Clare nestles on the gravel beach of a rivulet,
doffs his hat to write poetry and nods off in the heat.
He wakes to the stink of a hound and gamekeeper.
How to explain? 'I was only poaching your rimes, sir!'
when up pops Wisdom's cap bouncing along a hedgerow
followed by the Gypsy's tilting head, frame and pony:
'The might of noon to you, big man.' He sweeps his cap slyly.
The gamekeeper grins, the dog grins, gaping for his story.
After three hours gawping and cackling, the gamekeeper
strides home. Clare steals like a crake from the sedge,
Wisdom handing him his hat. 'No use seeking Gypsies, John.
When you want us, we make it impossible to find one.
When you're took up with other matters, we're everywhere.'
The river runs free and crooking among furze and reed-beds.

Fortune

they pertended to great skill both by cards and plants and by the lines
in the hand and moles and interpretations of dreams

'I envy your free-roving,' John Clare sighs to Wisdom Smith.
'To have the wide world as road and the sky and stars as your roof.'
'That bread in your mouth, brother,' butts in the Gypsy, 'is ours
because I bought it with my muscles and calluses this morning.
Man, the day gads off to market with the dawn and everything
sells itself under the sun: woods, trees, wildflowers and men.'
The Gypsy snicks a kettle from its crook: 'Do we not sell the hours
of our souls that we might be suffered to depart from them?'
Clare gazes at the fire. Wisdom cradles the poet's cup and stirs
and stares at the tea leaves: 'Our lives are whin upon this heath
whose growing makes one half of heaven and one half earth.
You desire an earthly heaven, John, and will find it in Helpston.
The leaves also say you are welcome to my fire – and to this cup.'
'You read a world from so little,' thinks Clare. And the Gypsy looks up.

The Gypsy's Evening Blaze

As soon as I got here the Smiths gang of gipseys came and encampd
near the town and as I began to be a desent scraper
we had a desent round of merriment for a fortnight

John Clare picks at Wisdom's tobacco pouch:
'Kindness flows like water in Christendom.
Wait – ' the poet writes 'while I pen a sketch.'
'I am no fit subject, friend,' warns Wisdom.
'To me, friend, this scene is wild and pleasing.'
'To you – *friend* – whose nose is nibbed with teasing.'
'To me – friend – so strong the scene prevades:
Grant me this life – thou spirit of the shades!'
'This is clishmaclaver. Cease feigning, John.'
The friends sit, hushed. Their pipes glare in the dark.
'Take my baccy but do not write me down.
Gifts given and ungiven are like words
forgiven and unforgiven. Word for word
they leave signs. I will not leave one boot mark.'

The Magic Stone

I became so initiated in their ways and habits
that I was often tempted to join them

Ramsons, sorrel and nettles gossip in a pot as Wisdom Smith
tells John Clare the tale of Stone Stew. 'A half-starved Gypsy
squats by his blaze. A gent idles up: "What broils here, young man?"
"This, Sir, is Stone Stew. Just boiling water and my magical stone.
It could taste angelic – given an onion." The gent offers an onion.
"Tatties, Sir, would saint the tang of it." The gent fetches a sackful.
The young man sips the soup. "A side of mutton would be heaven-sent."
And so on! – the gent brings lamb, loaves, butter, beer, and the broth
bubbles faster and fatter. "And, now Sir, taste of my enchantment!"
The Gypsy draws a ladle and loads a brimming bowl for the gentleman.
"Oh, this is the Lord of Stews," gasps the gent. "With one mineral
you have made alchemy. You must try some yourself." The bald stone
clatters in the drained pot as the gentleman heads home. The Gypsy
flings the rock' – Wisdom passes Clare a bowl – 'back on to the heath.'

Wisdom Smith Shows John Clare the Right Notes and the Wrong

If foky kek jins bute,
Mà sal at lende;
For sore mush jins chomany
That tute kek jins.

John Clare hails Wisdom Smith. The campfire leaps and licks
around a pot of hare stew. 'Timing again, poet,' notes Wisdom.
Afterwards, with quids of tobacco turning in their cheeks
the Gypsy lilts and spills notes on his fiddle. 'There are some – ,'
begins Wisdom, 'some that shall stay – nameless for shame –
who think our – music degraded when, in fact – it is the Deepest
of the Deep.' And the Gypsy slides his bow like a single scissored
screech to drive the point. Clare wakes up with a jolt and a jest,
'And there are plenty who say that about my poetry, Wisdom.
Why are the wrongest notes nearly always the rightest?'
Then Wisdom Smith plays him a melody no one alive has heard
not even the player, and Clare's mind clambers through crevasses
and canopies with only the Gypsy's fingertip holds for a guide.
'It is not deep, John,' says Wisdom finally, 'it is all surfaces.'

First Love

I met th[r]ee full stops or three professions of sincerity – my first was
a school affection – Mary J_____   I am ashamed to go on with the name

'You were saying, friend, you were children together,
larking with this girlfriend Mary in the church yard?'
John Clare flushes, 'We were playing at being birds,
fetching seeds and rosehips for our hidden brood.
I threw a walnut that struck Mary in the eye.
She wept and I hid my sorrow and my fancy
together under the shame of not showing regret
lest others might laugh it into love.' The Gypsy
stands, stretches and sets down another basket.
His palms and fingers bleed. 'This is the art of it.
If only we had craft like this for love, brother.'
Wisdom Smith squats in his nest of willow baskets,
each basket a perfect wicker creel. He twists and frets
the wands, not once glancing at the weeping poet.

Mad

Chichi nanéi dova toot. Jaw adré o shushenghi hevyaw.
Maur lendi ta hol lendi ti kokero. Porder ti pur ajàw.

Wisdom Smith smiles into his steaming bowl: 'March Hares
grow spooked in their bouts, so tranced by their boxing,
you can pluck them into a sack by the wands of their ears!'
John Clare hungers. He hugs his bowl and starts writing
on the surface of the stew with a spoon. 'Let the hare cool
on the night wind,' urges the Gypsy, 'Sip him but do not speak.'
The moon uncovers her face; the men slumber with minds awake –
for the stew has another mind and unpours the bowls into the pot,
shivering to stillness on a dying blaze until the broth is springwater
and hanks, ribs and lanky legs that dress themselves in bloody fur;
then a living hare leaps from the pot, dancing around Gypsy and poet
who, for this moment before morning, are asleep in the great spell
and who dream of striding backwards to Emmonsales Heath
to where mad hares spar and clash over the surface of the earth.

English

*The lil to lel oprey the kekkeno mushe's puvior
and to keir the choveno foky mer of buklipen and shillipen,
is wusted abri the Raioriskey rokkaring ker.*

'Your language, Gypsy,' mocks John Clare, 'is borrowed goods
or burglary. You smash up English to be hardly understood
then dispart under the drowk of your dark tongue's dossities.'
'And you?' smiles Wisdom, 'Folks say you dine on dictionaries
yet you remain a blank child, as foal-minded as any of my ponies –
tethered by a line, you still nose and slurp at flowers and clovers.'
But his friend is no longer listening to him: he dythers in miracles –
glimpt hedges are freshing with roosting starnels; a whirlipuff reels
as if something danced in it, and tazzles the grasses, ruffs the corn
where its wands are ramping, strows and stirtles the sprotes upon
the spirey blaze as the Gypsy progs it, forcing sparks with a stickle
to twinkle from the flaze. 'Gently now, brother,' urges the Gypsy,
'Warm your mind before you write of the things you see or hear.
They might not be of this world.' 'But my words are,' breathes Clare.

The Invisible Fair

let a gipsey drink out of her pail
To tell her her fortune

'Where do you stray, Wisdom, when you ride out?'
'Do you not see that foal? Horse-fairs, poet.'
'It moves with you wherever you are found?'
'Or follows – as a horse will nose the ground.'
'And where do you stay, friend, when you ride out?'
'See that foal rolling there? Horse-fairs, poet.'
'The art of travelling stirs in her step.'
'Arts of lightness – and knowing when to stop.'
'I heard some fair is nearing us tonight.'
'Some fair? – we are that fair. This is our site.'
'What might you sell to the Gentile people?'
'I sell them the moon trembling in a pail
or skim them fortune from a mirrored moon;
but would that cream savour of night or noon?'

Rime

*I usd to lye down under a tree in the Park and fall a sleep
and in the Autumn nights the rhyme usd to fall and cover me*

'The rime used to cover me, Wisdom,' crows John Clare,
'there was no escaping its poetry – it was everywhere.
It looked to me for life, were it a skeleton leaf in a trough
or a twig struck sidelong by the strivings of a tiny stream.
I would stare at them for hours – time was never enough.'
The Gypsy has not eaten for days; the poet is eating time.
'But the best of it, brother,' continues Clare, 'is the poetry
of what you have shown me, in the song-strings of the birds
or in the taut tongue of that bow,' Wisdom Smith rumbles,
making an O of his mouth and pressing it against his fingers.
'No, I am not yawning, John. I find if I hold my breath hard
I might devour the thin air. I have heard somewhere, brother,
that poets are like lizards and that you feed on light and air
whereas I would gladly,' the Gypsy eyes the poet, 'feast on lizards.'

The Hedgehog

I've seen it in their camps – they call it sweet
Though black and bitter and unsavoury meat.

John Clare is in a brown huff. Wisdom Smith is boxing the air,
prancing about him like a stoat. 'Poets are prickly creatures,'
jabs Wisdom, 'for all your talk of not having a second skin.'
'So Gypsies are whey-eyed, one-faced simpletons?' sulks Clare,
'Never an enigmatic word! Hearts fairly leaping off their sleeves!'
'I should skin you alive for that,' scowls the Gypsy, 'Slit your throat,
singe, gut and truss you like a pullet; wrap your poet's spiky pelt
in thumb-thick clay and plumb you into a fire-pit. Pluck clay
from your roasted trunk and serve up the dish called poetry:
all heart and squashy muscles.' Clare bunches himself into a ball:
'I would bind myself so tight, brother, I would never unroll.'
'If a hedgehog will not uncurl we pop him in a pot of hot water.'
The Gypsy springs at the poet. The poet rabbit-punches him in the gut.
Wisdom is winded and laughing. Clare grabs the kettle and runs for it.

Second Love

I first saw Patty going across the fields to her home... I clumb on top
of a dotterel to see which way she went till she was out of sight

The Gypsy snares a warren with a snigger of wires.
John Clare gropes around the coney holes for rhyme.
'You seem out of mind, poet, or out of time.
Are rhymes caught like a martin gaping for flies?
You to your work, brother-gaper, and me to mine
but no sobbing if supper is two bare bowls.'
They sally across the heathland to his camp. 'Soul's
Breath,' gasps Clare. A woman, waist-high in flowers.
A flash to a blazing. 'Do not stare at her,' cries Wisdom.
His friend climbs a doddered tree and clings to its crownless tip.
'You will seem a dotterel to that girl, brother,' caws the Gypsy,
'Loon-minded and limed on the branches of whim.'
John Clare is wordless. He is watching poetry from a tree.
A poem moving through wildflowers. A poem that will not stop.

A Spring Wife

if I had taken a step with out this caution
my love would have met a sudden end

The hedgerows itch with last summer's nests;
unwise saplings try out bright buds on their wrists.
John Clare is climbing the pollard to the sky.
'What do we see,' pants Clare, 'when we espy
a young woman cross a field?' 'You mean to say –
"What does John Clare, Poet and Lover", see? –
what I see are manners on the gallows,' sighs the Gypsy,
'We should go before we are caught and mocked.'
A thousand fieldfares lift off from the shocked
uplifted arms of an unleafed, woken oak.
'The Spring's spry wheels are rhyming on the roads,'
cries Wisdom, 'down the highway of every hedgerow;
and the birds from the North are steering with the sun.'
'Time,' shouts John, 'to declare.' And he climbs down.

Poems Descriptive of Rural Life and Scenery

my long smotherd affections for Mary revivd with my hopes
and as I expected to be on a level with her

Wisdom Smith reads; mouthing each murky word
and slitting his knife down uncut pages – *skrip-skrip*.
'If you will take it,' mumbles Clare, 'it is yours to keep.'
'And if I do not,' snips the Gypsy, 'it kindles firewood.'
Wisdom frowns: 'This – "mystery of common things" –
wagtails and nosegays – snowdrops and shepherds.
Who would buy and bow over – well – what he can read
by simply staring about the world? And – seeing
as most eyes are struck from their sockets by poverty,
who has the will to squander time on poetry?'
John Clare deals the cards: slap-slap-slap-slap, slap.
'I fear, John, you are writing for squires and their ladies.'
The poet nods at no one. He flips his cards face-up.
'No,' smiles Clare, 'I am not. I am writing – for my Mary.'

A Steeple-Climber

You must jib by your jibben: and if a base
se tukey you must chiv lis tuley.

The Blue Bell Inn on Woodgate in the small hours after Time.
'I was thinking,' slurs John Clare, 'now I can turn a poem
I might turn to an even thornier art.' 'Like hedge-laying
you mean?' winks Wisdom, 'There is more coin in snedding
than blotting.' 'My friend, there are men of merit and name
who pleach whole hedges of words. They call it criticism.
What I want' – Clare pounds the deal table – 'is more scale.'
Mishearing, the landlord stumps across with a brimming jug.
'I just mean,' stammers John, 'to be taken to heart by those men.
I have been a steeple-climber all my life. Such is my poor pen.'
John glares into his ale. Wisdom flickers a finger toward the ceiling.
He blows a slow column of smoke up. Everybody in the pub
stares and sees what the gypsy has made. '*There* is the steeple.
This' – Wisdom circles his arm – 'this is the church and the people.'

A Picture of Eternity Drawn in Crayons

*Meklis juggal, ta av acoi, ma kair
the rye kinyo with your gudli.*

John Clare returns from The Hall, one hand in his pocket.
The twenty-pound note is still real. Wisdom is opposite:
'Wealth meets the world as smooth as a bowling green,
easy as a cushion. When do we have time for games, John?'
'Can you not rejoice for me this once, Gypsy?' 'For money?
Every time I drink and eat by it. But what is served before
or after puts my stomach on edge.' 'Then let us translate it,'
says Clare, 'into what comes between.' At the Exeter Arms
the men relax into rounds, pies and Beggar My Neighbour.
'I had to read to his Lordship, Wisdom, from my book of poetry
and his Lordship listened.' His friend smiles. Clare has to get home.
He moves to pay, but the Gypsy has cleared the slate. 'Flattery
writes such fawning phrases, John, but time wipes them away
like a picture of eternity drawn in crayons.' 'No, Wisdom.'

Wisdom Smith Shakes John Clare's Hand

Does tute jin the Romano drom of lelling the wast?
Avali, prala.
Sikker mande lis.
They kairs it ajaw, prala.

Clare pricks out poems under hedges when out of work or late,
crooked down in ditches beside the scribbling pondskaters;
whirligig beetles jiggle under the held stares of hoverflies
their tiny brains fizzing and misfiring. Wisdom Smith clicks a gate.
John jumps to his feet fearing the landlord's gamekeepers.
'Do you know the Gypsy way of taking the hand?' 'Aye, brother.'
'Show it to me,' asks Wisdom 'They do it so, brother.' Clare
cocks a thumb as if palm were a gun; aims it below the wrist
with a soft pressure a horse knows as a stroke of trust.
'You are leaving again.' 'Too many fairs and affairs to hold me.
You be easier on yourself, John, and on that pen – go gently.
Those things, they can turn when you least expect them.'
His horses stamp and blow. Wisdom throws back his arm
as John Clare clumps home. 'They does it so, brother.'

A Prayer

Yov kairs mandi te sov telé adré o chorengri poovyaw.
Yov leleth mandi posh-rig o shookár paani.

John Clare kicks at the corpse of a campfire. The ash-motes
blush in the breeze. The poet tears a taper from his notes,
lights his long pipe, and reads over the torn page, whispering:
I feel a beautiful providence ever about me as my attendant deity
she casts her mantle about me when I am in trouble to shield me
from it   she attends me like a nurse when I am in sickness
puts her gentle hand under my head to lift it out of pains way
lays it easy by laying hope for my pillow   she attends to my
every weakness when I am doubting like a friend and keeps me
from sorrow by showing me her pictures of happiness – and offering
them up to my service   she places herself in the shadow
that I may enjoy the sunshine and when my faith is sinking
into despondency she opens her mind as a teacher to show
me truth and give me Wisdom when I had it

WORLD'S EYE

I found the poems in the fields
And only wrote them down

John Clare

The Boy and the Wren

In as much as anything is anything
this is an invisible universe, yet particles
in his fingers swirl within Saturn's rings,
they fly in the eye of Jupiter and arc
across the Great Galaxy of Andromeda.
This is not poetry. It is mathematics
in as much as anybody is listening.

In as much as anybody is listening
the lorikeets and redpolls trill
imperceptibly as if the sound
of our planet had swung to zero.
Nothing is happening and no one
and nothing is calling and calling
in as much as anyone is listening.

In as much as anyone is listening
the boy vanishes through a door
while his parents shout and snarl
the words none should hear
while a child is in hearing.
This is not history. It is every evening
in as much as anybody is listening.

In as much as anybody is listening
the boy grows tired with running
when a bush bursts open before him
to reveal a wren rampant in song
and everything is forgotten
that needs to be forgotten
in as much as anything is forgotten.

On Not Rushing at Waterfalls

I did
I did not want   not want
  to rush   rush upon
  the waterfalls   so I took
   a footpath   going up the side of
  of the hill   to catch a glimpse
  of them   first   first from there.
   The scene   suggested adventure
  and inspiration   for verses
   not a sense   of desolation.
   Climbing I saw   I saw one of
  one of the falls   one of the falls
   streaming down   like a sheet of thick
  silvery-white paper. The thought of it
having rolled down like   that for centuries…
  The sound of the falls   grew louder and nearer.
In front of the waterfalls I felt caressed as a child
  in its mother's arms. The more I watched it
   The more
   I watched it
  the more I had
the impression that
it was not moving at all
  not moving
   at all

Walking from Barden Bridge to the Valley of Desolation up Posforth Gill

Fugitive

When he had kair'd the moripen, he plastrar'd adrey the wesh,
where he gared himself drey the hev of a boro, puro rukh

He'd shot a policeman and scarpered into this wood
where he'd hid himself in the hollow of a great oak
and in that chilled chamber under the toes of the tree
the searching helicopters could not spy his burning body.

He had the handgun braced by his palm and ready,
buried himself for days, waking to bats and moths,
gnawing at roots for carbs, wringing ferns for water.
So rage fell from him and he pawed his way to a river.

A woodcock swooped and roddered. The moon froze silver.
He slept night and day among the quillwort by the river.
Moths and midges. Their movement made shadow softer
as search lamps sapped him, as the Taser Unit crept closer:
sparrowhawk to the sparrow, as flycatcher to the fly,
as light to the cribs of larvae under the quillwort's canopy.

& Son

Jack Vardomescro could del oprey dosta to jin sore,
oprey the mea-bars and the drom-sikkering engris.

They said Jack Cooper could read enough to know
all that was upon the milestones and the signposts.
All that he did not know he borrowed from his boy.
What the boy did not know Jack paid no mind to.

That boy was a squirrel with books and papers from schools,
nineteen schools from thirty-odd stopping places. The boy
could pluck and crack knowledge like acorn nuts for winter
knowing or near knowing where food might lie hidden.

If a thing hooked the boy's mind like a burr it was never lost
as nothing is, rag and bone. All fathers are fools.
All fathers are fools to their fathers, but to their sons
those fathers were sixty seasons they grew wilder in
before they took to trade and hauled its ragged wisdom.
It is why *Jack Cooper & Son* farm the soft world for iron.

Hawker

The nav they dins lati is Bokht drey Cuesni
because she rigs about a cuesni which sore the rardies
when she jals keri is sure to be perdo of chored covers.

The widow's shawl is alive with puppies plugging each pocket;
her knapsack nodding with pegs, heather and trinkets.
The name the Gypsies give her is Luck in a Basket
because she carts about a creel which every night
when she heads home is stuffed with stolen brands
as though goods had the will to leap to her sideways
from coat, car, carrier bag or window ledge.

She will have none of your tricks, not if you buy from her.
The market-men shift sulking from behind their stands.
They lean staring from the stalls, knot their red arms.
Yet the name they sling her is the last name to their own.

Later she dozes by her basket under a drowsing hedge
away from the campfire. This is the home the Gypsies give her.
Yellowhammers tug horsehair from stars of barbed wire.

Leaf
Leaf litter
Leaf-lit Leaf-lit
Leaf light Leaf light
Leaf fight Leaf fight
Leaf flight Leaf flight
Leaf letters Leaf letters
Leaf laughter Leaf laughter
Leaf slaughter Leaf slaughter
Leaf slaughter Leaf slaughter
Leaf laughter Leaf laughter
Leaf letters Leaf letters
Leaf flight Leaf flight
Leaf fight Leaf fight
Leaf light Leaf light
Leaf-lit Leaf-lit
Leaf litter
Leaf

Walking off public footpath in Strid Wood

Leaf litter
Leaf–lit Leaf–lit
Leaf light Leaf light
Leaf fight   Leaf fight
Leaf flight   Leaf flight
Leaf letters   Leaf letters
Leaf   laughter   Leaf   laughter
Leaf   slaughter Leaf   slaughter
Leaf   slaughter Leaf   slaughter
Leaf   laughter   Leaf   laughter
Leaf letters   Leaf letters
Leaf flight   Leaf flight
Leaf fight   Leaf fight
Leaf light Leaf light
Leaf–lit

Walking upstream from Strid Wood to Embsay

Barden Tower

I have heard a tourist claim this view
as though she had bought it at cost –
an expensive mirror. Unseen and ornately
ivy throws its ropes across the leaf-litter
shifting a forest's massive furniture;

the moss robes veil the thrones
of fallen oaks; trees flare with lichen;
Autumn smashes rainbows across
the woodland floor. You may never
have seen these trees more brilliantly

than when you turned your eyes
to that hunting lodge and sensed the light
kindle a million leaf mirrors.
In his woods near Lake Tuusula
Jean Sibelius shaped symphonies

from the speech of trees; firs bowed
violins while his swans sailed, keening.
Before his death a solitary swan
veered over and made him her own.
I am close to you who once shared this view.

This is not my sky, my flight, my words. This is not a mirror.

Walking from Embsay back to Barden Bridge

Pipping

It is living nests that could introduce a phenomenology of the actual nest, of the nest found in natural surroundings, and which becomes for a moment the centre – the term is no exaggeration – of an entire universe...

Gaston Bachelard, *The Poetics of Space*

Although rendering bird voices in writing inevitably is inexact and personal, a serious effort has been made to convey what is typical for each call by trying to select the letters and style of writing which are most apt.

Collins Bird Guide

Long-Tailed Tit

restlessly moving parties utter loud trisyllabic, sharp 'scrih-scrih-scrih'

A nursery ball
with a world inside
blown through branches
– bauble, with a tail
peals in its nest-
bell of lichen

Wren

metallic ringing notes and trills: 'zitrivi-si **svi-svi-svi-svi-svi** zivüsu **zü-zü-zü-zü** si-**zirrrrrrr svi-svi-svi** siyu-**zerrrrrr** sivi'

```
        that
        ratt-
          ling              hedge
          has             a heart
          the copper    heart-
        beat of a bush
        from which
        it  bursts
          the
          2nd-small-
        est
          god-
                send
```

Chaffinch

bright, loud almost rattling verse... the whole terminating in a
flourish, 'Zitt-zitt-zitt-zitt-sett-sett-sett-chatt-chiteriidia'

```
      whose call
      is a cricketer bustling up
                          to bowl
      who hurtles to the crease
      then releases

                              the
                              ball
```

48

Dunnock

an irresolute shuttling or patchwork of sounds

Trust the plainest of birds
with the sweetest calls
to carry them under cover
lest they fall into the claws
of a hoopoe or golden plover.

Greenfinches

sometimes the wheezing song is woven into the musical song

or   they are precision
      instruments
      for opening seed hearts

      jade lanterns
      on a bough –
      sweet-hearts and pair-bonds

or   emerald
      lamps lit
      over a seed cage

      they lime-light the branches,
      bright
      pears or goosegogs

no   green more greener
      or finch
      more finchier

greenness a thousand times more green
Dorothy Wordsworth, *Journal*

Willow Tit

1–2 short notes followed by 2–4 lower, hoarse, harsh, drawn out
notes, 'zi-zi **taah taah taah**'. Also fine conversational 'zi' notes

black cap
   & black bib
world's eye
   on the wold
skids side
   slides skywards
bright ear
   of the heard wood
hearing
   in zizigzags
sounding
   the iron twigs'
precision
   xylophones

Twite

fat trills, buzz-notes, electric twitters – the hedgerow shred from inside by scissors

Were it not for
   the slight upended
twite suspended
   below that lancing spray
of elder blossom
   then the light that slid
through my eye
   last night, that told
the twite's call
   within an ear of sight
may well, may not,
   may never, be remembered.

Great Tits

a simple seesawing ditty with slightly mechanical intonation, '**ti**-ta, **ti**-ta, **ti**-ta' or trisyllabic and with different stress, 'ti-ti-**ta** ti-ti-**ta** ti-ti-**ta**'

high-wire acrobats
of our bird-feeder's
three-ring circus

clingers   climbers
ringers   rhymers

they call for teachers
for teachers

& have nothing
to learn

Olive-backed Pipit

to Julia Wheadon at Totleigh Barton

song as Tree Pipit's, but the verses are often a bit shorter, the voice softer and
higher, the tempo fast throughout, and the trills are drier

This chirr-
    ing chatterer
  sends herself
    to Siberia
      never speci-
        fies snowfall
          in her sweet
      calls for fear
          (she sings dryly)
        of our pity or
      (softer *yet*, *yet*, *yet*)
    of frost spinning
    its white lies
  over and under
her airs   her verses

Deserted Nest Box

The wood birds
are now in exile

for the white
time is here:

skulls of leaf litter,
a fledgling frost,

bleached tree wings.
They might call

again next year.

A Butterfly Emerges from the Poems of E.B.

Tousled Cleopatra –
a Clouded Yellow Butterfly

eases her limbs
from the page's leaves,

from those bedspreads,
a pulpy scrim

cocooned, uncrowned
among the rinds

of a cold spring
(living hand

on this paper,
nudging her warm);

she half-arcs her
height to heaven –

flamenco-clapping
the earth, trips

a tattering
flight path to strum

on a sunned
stone sternly;

flexes two full
fans until on

one updraft
her grace flares

from that anvil.

Fruit Fly

Awake and hum their tiny songs anew,
And climb the totter-grass and blossom's stem

As if I had
scaled a Redwood,
teetered blindly
on its tipping spire,
Drosophila –
you ascend
your gradual
gradual grass tower.
Your weight wakes
no movement.
Weightless as if
stepping out to space
you reach its rim,
that razor. You stroke
the scythes on a
grass blade's tip.
You shuffle, shiver
sure in your stance,
stitch your six sticky feet
to the perch
of its peak.
Drosophila, your mind
is moving, a fleck
in a pinspeck.
You flick out your fans,
decant fresh temperature
through the burnished
canals in your wings.
Only then with your
systems satisfied,
the poise planted
and perfect –
your wings fire up, fizz,
flicker frantic flirting
gestures, flinging frequencies

beyond any hearing but your own
yet you are yodelling
across a million million
million peaks. A swallow
skimming the lawn may
yawn towards you but
you are no larger than a life.

Fight

after Lorca

Noon buzzes with blowflies,
the microcircuitry of cicadas.
Two gypsy tribes ride into a ravine,
ramming into each other
the bull's head of their battle
smashing about the coppice
stamping, slicing like a rutting bull
mounting his own horns.
Two widows watch weeping
from beside an olive net.
The gypsies are down or out,
nine are dying and dead:
Juan Antonio spews scarlet lilies,
the spume of pomegranates.
Sunlight slits the ridden
and the riders to silhouettes.
The gypsies dream of snow
and bandages as they bleed
and sweat. The women
crouch low. Angels of dust
eavesdrop from above.
A mob boss and his henchmen
step out from the olive grove.
'Gentlemen, you can trust
these people to do this
again and again. Four
Roma leaders are dead
and five more of their best men.
These fools do our job for us.
Finish them and fleece them.'

Ballad of the Moon, Moon

El aire la vela, vela.
El aire la está velando.

after Lorca

A pettelengra boy whacks petalos on his anvil.
  The moon slides into his smithy, bright as a borì.
The boy cannot stop himself staring. The moon
  releases her arms in flames of flamenco,
her sweet dress slipping from one shoulder.
  'Nash nash, choon, nash nash, choon, choon.
If the Rom catches you he will splice your zi.
  He will smelt your soul for miriklè and vongustrì.'
The moon smiles, 'Chavvo, let me kur my kellipen.
  By the cherris the gyppos come, they will find you
poggadi on the anvil with your biddi yokkers lelled.'
  'Nash nash, choon, nash nash, choon, choon.
Run for it, moon, run away, moon, fair moon.
  I can hear the hooves of my horse masters hammering.'

'Chavvo, muk me be. Don't pirro upon my pawni
  ringi so rinkana.' The drumskin of the plains thrums
with hoof-strokes. The boy backs across the smithy.
  Horse masters hove through the night-tree
a forest in slow motion, bronze and dream.
  Bronze and dream are the Roma, their eyes sky-high,
their gaze lances through walls of world and smithy.
  But the moon dances her prey to the snare of a mirror.
She hauls the pettelengra o kolè dyoonaste to the pliashka.
  The gypsies ride at her trailing veils, her mokkadi doovàki.
The wind whips by, wraps the moon in her purlènta.
  It wraps that bride, the moon, the moon, *barval, bevvali!*

Romani: **pettelengra**: blacksmith; **petalos**: horseshoes; **borì**: bride; **nash**: run
away!; **choon**: moon; **Rom**: Romanies; **zi**: heart, soul; **miriklè**: necklaces;
vongustrì: rings; **Chavvo**: boy; **kur my kellipen**: do my dancing; **cherris**: time;
poggadi: broken; **biddi**: tiny; **yokkers**: eyes; **lelled**: locked up; **muk**: let/allow;

pirro: tread; **pawni**: whiteness; **ringi**: dressed; **rinkana**: spruce; **o kolè dyoonaste**: beyond, in the other world; **pliashka**: Romani ceremony before wedding; **mokkadi**: dirty; **doovàki**: veil; **purlènta**: silk headkerchief; **barval, bevvali**: wind.

Pallid Swift

for Gabriel

How many species of crossbow,
families of boomerang,
genera of scimitars
fling weightlessly on thermals
this Mediterranean morning?
Swifts are not for counting, so sly
in their air-slid, scissored, flycatching
flight-patterns. They swim our eyes
to vertigo. Swat with their gape.
Swoon through alleys between
wheel-blurs of motorbikes. Severed
from earth from the egg, blinking
from the muck of nestcups
with all air for instructor, then
air as taught: to bend to the well
of the fledged fall, plunge, sprawl
and flicked brace of a wingspan
that never ceases straining taut-sprung
except to craft nestcups or die.
                                        So
this fallen Pallid Swift, wings locked
full-tilt, flopped on a paving stone,
dropped from that sky-high where
and why of noon-light and updraft
and high-fly. But we were elated,
for a few seconds we chanced
on nearness while her wide, still-
soaring eyes flickered, nictitated
with shock, shadow and slow
gravity. With weight. With
the load-lifted promise spent.
All we knew was to launch her,
to pitch her like a rag plane
across a runway of air and hope
muscle-memory or memory

would jump-start the wings' rotors
refired from her pulled motor.
But she sputtered. Toppled.
And I unfolded the lie
as we palmed her soft under
a palm tree's poor shade, she,
still blinking, still flying, still gaping, still soaring,
uncounted that morning.

Corfu Town

Foxes, Swans, Starlings

An Arctic Fox paces far into the north
touching mountains with his fur
so that sparks strike off into
the sky as starlings. A throng
of swans arrows far north
flapping exhausted, entrapped
in sea-ice; they beat their wings,
their reflections release an aurora
borealis of starlings. Charged photons
can ignite them; to prove the story
a model world was electrified
with a magnetic field, and they rose
fire-dancing in the sky,
foxes, swans, starlings.

Marriage Vows of a Rom to a Gadji

To all of you at this pliashka, we are one
Until the shadows steal our horses home.
To thee, romni, lightest lace across thy kocsh,
For the treasures of lon and gold marò.
Break the bold marò, Borì – salve it
In the blood and salt upon thy knee.
Share this salt, this bread, this blood.
Let us leap low over the candles' glow.
Mi dèhiba, I feed thee and thou wilt feed me
Even as our hearts slow, our tresses sewn with suy.
Our unlike hands will untangle. We shall
Gather up kookoochìn for your balà.
Sorì simensar sì mèn, we cry as one.
All who are with us are ourselves.

Rom: Romani man; **Gadji**: Non-Roma woman; **pliashka**: Romani ceremony preceding the 'abiav' or wedding; **romni**: wife; **kocsh**: knee; **lon**: salt (n); **marò**: bread; **Borì**: bride; **mi dèhiba**: my beloved; **suy**: grey; **kookoochìn**: snowdrops; **balà**: hair; **Sorì simensar sì mèn**: We are all one; all who are with us are ourselves.

Sessile and Strid

DESCANT ON OAK AND WHARFE
Oak calligramme

As tree is to this river
so the Wharfe's weather so the rain's seed
so the rain's bud   so the rain's bloom
so the spring's root   so the spring's shoot   so the spring's stock
so the spring's stems   so the beck's spray   so the beck's sprigs
so the beck's brake   so the beck's branch   so the river's boughs
so the river's vines   so the river's fronds   so the river's palms
so the Strid's wall   so the Strid's warp
so the Strid's spooring so the Strid's roaring
and so hoving to the oak's shore.
As river is to this tree
so the oak's quay
the bark's ark the bark's brook
the bark's wakes the root's wades
the root's spate   the root's race
the root's wells   the trunk's prow
the trunk's oar the trunk's mast
the trunk's wall
the branch's waves
the branch's becks
the branch's rills
the branch's tides
leaf's flood
leaf's shoals
leaf's skiffs
leaf's shore
so the water's roar.

Walking and climbing from The Strid up through Strid Wood

THE POET

I might have said my first wife and first love
and first everything

John Clare, Notebook

The Pen

& if friendship [   ] you would win it
& should black guard fate leave us with [   ]
I am yours to [   ] in it

John Clare writes air between his words. He senses his friend
beside him [   ]. But Wisdom has wended
below the horizon to an earth beyond Northamptonshire.
The poet lets his pen fall. It rolls on a bearing to the door.
Clare follows it with his eye. The nib tuts over the stone floor
writing its way across a world as if held by an invisible child.
It pricks at his knee with its one claw, a kitten pawing to be held.
John reaches down; then howls as the pen stabs his hand.
He yanks at the thing. Flesh-suction grips and the wound tightens
like an anemone of ink. By now the room and world are in a spin,
one around the other – a gyroscope buzzing inside a gyroscope.
'If I could win a name through poetry and sacrifice friendship
for that prize' – the pen rattles loose. John sinks to the floor.
He senses his poem beside him [   ].

An Olive-Green Coat

a new olive green coat a color which I had long aimed at and for which I was
measured already ere I left home expecting to be able to pay for it but a accident
happened in the way which prevented me   the gipseys   etc etc

John Clare longs to look the part, the part a poet can play
– no part labourer. He stares at a tailor's display, his money
gone, his hard hands numb with the vision of further toils.
He stumps over five bridges, each of them tedious as hills
on the elm-heavy miles between Stamford and Helpston.
Langley Bush blurs with caravans. John dashes to the atching tan
waving and shouting. 'Hark!' cries Wisdom Smith to his crew,
'Who here has lost a hound? – for there is one on the avenue
for the taking.' The poet comes gambolling up. The Gypsies
cackle quietly into the crook of their arms. Clare fumes: 'Already –
even before we might rekindle friendship – I fall under attack.
I grieved for you – brother. I should have saved myself the bother.'
The Gypsy rummages through a sack. A yaffle's pulse of jade;
cuffs of crimson silk lining. 'I thought, you know, John, for your back.'

Romani: **atching tan**: stopping place

Bender

the next day when I passd the place the gable end
we had sat under was down and a heap of rubbish

'Let us relate our stocious tales of last night!' John Clare howls
and Wisdom hoots at the memory of them fleeing – filching
a lanthorn and a flagon of ale then dossing and drinking
until dawn in a ramshackle shack which, by the morning,
had completely caved in around them. 'We were like barn owls
on a beam,' cries the poet, 'outstaring, upstanding!' 'You, brother,'
tuts the Gypsy, 'are still drunk or, any road, drunk on some idea.'
'It is the poetry of night, Wisdom. That is the very barn you Gypsies
used for your reveries and romancing.' 'It is where we slept, brother.
But it is a singing summer. We will wind willows into benders.'
'Poetry is in season,' laughs John, 'Rooms woven from wound wood
are like rooms of woven words.' Wisdom looks at Clare – hard.
'Poetry is not everything. You know that, John,' smiles the Gypsy.
'You are wrong,' dances Clare. 'Everything. Everything is poetry.'

My Children

Where I lived with my children the whole summer long

The Gypsy progs the slow fire and listens.
'I do not write,' John Clare tells Wisdom Smith,
'my fingers founder on raising a pen;
'my eye blackens the parlour and the hearth;
'all I love; hedges and fields stand silent;
'I have no pride in working or in life;
'I no longer have a friend in yourself;
'I have no friend in myself.' 'I had children,'
breathes Wisdom, 'all three boys now dead or grown.
I was a boy myself when fathering them.
Those boys.' The Gypsy rises and stares at John:
'Don't – don't stamp on yourself.' 'Every moment
I stamp on myself. Were poems children
I should stamp their lives out.' 'Then do not make them.'

Worlds

It is pleasant as I have done today to stand
... and notice the objects around us

'There is nothing in books on this,' cries Clare.
'I do not read, brother,' states Wisdom smiling,
'for I will not bother with Mystery.
Worlds move underfoot. Where lives Poetry?
Look,' hums Wisdom Smith, 'in the inner domes
of ghost orchids – how the buzzing rimers
read light with their tongues; or in this anthill –
nameless draughtsmen crafting low rooms, drawing
no fame – except the ravening yaffle,
or fledgy starlings bathing in their crawl.
I see these worlds – lit worlds. I live by them.'
The wood-ants sting. John Clare shifts foot to foot:
'I did not know you gave me any thought.'
'This? All this – is nothing, John,' laughs Wisdom.

The Spared

we heard the bells chime but the field was our church

John Clare is chewing his hat and raving: 'My wife supposed
me to be at church when I was with you, Wisdom; the reverend
imagined I was with my wife, tending her ague.' 'Yet you chose
this Sabbath morning,' smiles the Gypsy, 'to slumber by my blaze.
Your snores cheered the Sunday Schoolers out on a nature ramble;
their crow-toed Captain twitched his switch at your cadaver! –
but thought better, your children being counted amid his crew…'
'No, no, no, no, no,' mouths Clare, 'my five lambs? with the preacher?'
The poet peers into the dry well of his hat, feeling for his brains:
'I must rime reams about his churches: Glinton spire and Helpston;
then bestow the work – on my wife! I will be spared. All might be well.'
Clare whets his pen and sweats out the poem. Wisdom Smith frowns:
'Do you think, John, your people are that starved for your good word?'
'I wrote a poem about your people!' 'Hm,' amens the Gypsy, 'Spare us.'

Hedge-layers

Solitary persons are sideing up the hedges and thrusting the brushwood in the thin places and creeps which the swine made from one ground or field into another and stopping gaps made by gleaners and labourers

Sheep scuttle from pasture to pasture following their green god.
John and Wisdom go gapping-up: one man on the cattle-side,
one among barley; both friends shin-deep in sliding cherry mud.
Their billhooks snicker as they sned the stems and the stubs
weep sap. They have toiled since dawn. It is time for their bait.
'It is time for debate,' shouts the Gypsy over the hazel hethering.
'We weave the pleachers later.' John Clare kneels at the feet
of the hedgerow. He sheep-shoves through one of the breaks;
his body will not follow. Wisdom smiles and goes on speaking:
'The hedges of hawthorn yearn to become trees. They grow
with their young legs splayed. They sway with ripening buds.
A pleacher reaches for its root through its bark and sapwood
which is all in our cut and our angle and our taking of its toe.
Lie fallow there, poet, and you will grow young with the hedgerow.'

The Souls

Far spread the moory ground...

'Hark,' chaffs Wisdom, 'while I show you the craft! –
each rock's snug square on its brothers' shoulders;
their boys – those bitty stones – they huddle under.
Capstones? They're the boss. Boss-stones man the edge.
Now you choose the stones, brother, while I graft.'
Clare stares over the vanished field of sedge.
'It's for a wage, John. What is land to me?
The road is my pocket. Yours is poetry.
When winter comes it is walling feeds you up.
High walls shield you for when you have to stop.'
But Clare has downed his tools. He strides unseen
under the wall, beneath the moors and sky
below the scum of ditches, and between
his soul and his old soul's following eye.

Lapwings

... four eggs of dingy dirty green
Deep blotched with plashy spots of jockolate stain

Hedge-laying, ditch-delving, John Clare has not written for weeks.
His friend hefts clay beside him. Lapwings stare past them
as if they were landowners. The Gypsy unbends. His shovel arm
shivers as if broken. 'Like a Pie-wipe from her eggs,' Wisdom winks,
'I draw off that stoat by conjured weakness.' But the foreman spies him.
Clare gathers his things, grumbling: 'We have no right to be draining
these ancient wading pools.' Later, the Gypsy rides up to him singing.
'Our lives, brother-delver, are nothing to that of England. Pee-wees
will inherit the earth long after you or his Lordship are mouldering.
As for the boss-man, well, after you left he kept yakking foolishness
until I said, "if you goes on I'll hit you a hot 'un on the nose".
I dropped him with my words, poet.' A sun-shaft shakes loose.
Glory. Wonder. Wisdom reaches under his saddlebags for a rifle.
'John Clare, I know a hangar where the conies are as fat as foals.'

Hunters

Dikas mendi kater dulla staani. Yon pooderenna
lendi te lendi yogomegri.

Wisdom Smith whets his knife; John Clare oils his tongue.
Starlight reaches them after a million years of flying.
'The night makes a promising page,' murmurs Wisdom,
'You trance your rhymes like moths under your lanthorn.
I trap the nibbling deer with wires and soundless blade.'
'When I was a boy,' shivers John Clare, 'Why, I dared
never look up in my wanderings; my eye ever glegging
under my hat at every stir of a leaf or murmur of wind.'
'Poor John,' whistles the Gypsy, 'a quaking thistle would
make you swoon.' 'Truth is, Wisdom, a thistle still could!'
laughs the poet. And the friends snort and drink to the night.
Clare snores beneath his blanket. Wisdom rises from the earth.
Their fire is all there is to show. Orion stares down on the heath.
He searches for their world with a slow sword of light.

A Bivouac

The gipseys in matters of religion
are not so unfeeling as may be imagind

'I love it when fieldfares flicker and chinking redwings steer
between stars': John Clare gazes up from the fire
tuning his stare to starlight. Wisdom hushes him, 'Brother,
we cannot nap on the wing like the swifts or the swallows.
There is legwork at dawn down the limekilns at Casterton.'
'The night lets slip her mind, Gypsy,' starts Clare, 'She hears
in light. The dumb, dark matter we conceive of as night
is where we hide or are hidden from the poetry of her thought...'
'And there is the poetry of dreams,' growls the Gypsy – 'John,
when you say her, you do mean him, don't you? As in Him?'
'I do not care what to think,' Clare mumbles to Wisdom.
'Henceforth,' declares the poet, drowsing, 'I shall not think twice.'
'No, you shall think twice. Twice.' – and the Gypsy rolls his eyes
or his eye rolls him; as he turns the world, or the world turns him.

Lime-burners

I had a great desire myself of joining the Smiths Crew and a young fellow
that I workd with at a lime kiln did join with them

A coal-line of long-dead trees; a stone-line of ancient reefs:
John Clare shovels in the limestone and the lumps of coal.
'Limestone was living stone,' lectures the Gypsy, 'it was coral
crammed undersea, and – see! – veiled in fractured coal are leaves;
it is life upon life, John.' 'I wish they made the lines of a poem –
for I cannot rime here.' 'A "lazy kiln" you are,' huffs Wisdom,
'jumping from job to job with your fires blazing then fading.
You want the kiln-money for riming; I need it for my roving.'
One day to load; three to fire-through; two to cool; and another
to rake the quicklime, burning a living reef into blinding powder.
'What's dead-burned is gone to bad,' bellows the kiln-owner,
'Dump those riddlings. Just barrow them down to the riverside.'
And the little river wound along a sloping meadow northward
losing its name and its whitening waters into strangers' streams.

The Ring

*I thought my first wife lay on my left arm and somebody took her away
from my side which made me wake up rather unhappy.*

The Flowerpot Inn at Tickencote. The lime-burners slake
the Sunday through, dousing quicklime from their lungs.
Wisdom coughs; John Clare mutters: 'Again we are owls –
hacking up pellets of ancient bone and stone. Pour me a lake
of beer to plash my innards of dust.' 'Lime torches our tongues,
brother,' wheezes Wisdom – 'no lake large enough for a poet's.'
His friend charges him. The Gypsy dodges. John goes sprawling.
'Why, brother-labourer, what is askew with your bearing?
Why do you spill in the sawdust with skidding feet?
The flags of a common inn are no place for a poet.'
John Clare stops larking. He stares weeping at the walls:
'My wedding ring is lost, gone in sawdust or the kiln coals.
I was never married, Wisdom, not unless I were wed
to my first wife and first love and first everything. Yet she is dead.'

Last Love

I thought as I awoke somebody said 'Mary' but nobody was near –
I lay down with my head towards the north

'John, you are wed to Patty. "Patty of the Vale" –
you called her that last time I stopped at Helpston.
A thing made cannot be unmade, brother.'
The oak's leaves jostle and whisper in their rust.
None wishes to be the first to fall. The migrations
when they come will see all fly down on one gust.
Wisdom Smith gathers acorns in a clattering pail
while his best friend smokes and stares into hell.
'She is no maid next to Mary,' murmurs Clare.
'This will go nowhere, John, except lunacy.'
'Then we will stride there, but I will walk with Mary.'
The sap, sensing winter, prepares their skeletons
drawing the food from the tree's starving cells,
ruling that the rain runs silent in their walls.

A Flitting

... the world's end was at the edge of the horizon
and that a day's journey was able to find it.

John Clare is moving house. 'You might as well be evicting
your own heart and mind,' cries Wisdom. 'You are bricks, mortar
and poetry. All are bound. You know that from your lime-kilning.'
'Let us not quarrel. My patron chose. I have no choice, Wisdom.'
The Gypsy curses under his breath. 'If you had been cast forth
for some badness I would have stayed silent. It makes me mad
you choose to go, and to go along with some rich man's fad...'
'As if you, Gypsy, have not stridden three miles down one road
then the next day three or thirty miles, one way or t'other,
from whim or work or weather...' Clare heaves the last load
on the wagon, wraps ropes around the lot and turns to Wisdom:
'I am moving three miles, my friend, not to the edge of the earth.'
Wisdom Smith shouts through the dust kicked up by iron rims:
'That is not what they say in these parts about Northborough'.

Blea

Ploughed fields and meadow lands are blea
In hedge and field each restless twig
Is dancing on the naked tree

The poet stares at the moor. The Gypsies have flown
with the dawn. Their wheels rasp and creak through
the songless air. John is John and all alone.
Larks start up from the brown grass in the meadow
and Clare takes note – *with a couple of flutters and flights*
he drops out of sight as suddenly again into the grass…
His pen becomes an eye – *The rawky mornings*
now are often frosty – and the grass and wild herbs
are covered with rime as white as a shower of snow.
There is a pair of harrows painted red standing on end
against the thorn hedge and an old plough stands
on beam ends against a dotterel tree. Immense flocks
of starnels settled on an ash tree in the orchard
and when they took wing it was like a roll of thunder.

Tenant of Leaves & Flowers & Glossy Stalks

In Spring the leafing hedges brings to my memory the times when
I anxiously rambld about them at leisure hours hunting the birds nest
and pootys and I cannot help peeping among them still

The brambles are barbed shut, a sharp school
for spiders. John Clare's boy steers his fingers
to the hush where he hazards a nest slumbers
cradled among spines. He misses it, howls,
and waves at the wind as if scalded, the chicks'
beaks boiling up in their saucepan of sticks.
One baby rolls over trembling on the nest's
brim. His brothers shoulder him out and splay
their gapes. The boy stares at their silhouettes
then he retches. The nest falls silent. The boy
remembers his father's blank stare. He stretches.
Thorns think nothing of his arm. He clutches,
winces as chicks jab the worms of his fingers.
A gift for his mad father. And the scars for show.

Woodsmanship

*the spring had taken up her dwelling in earnest she has covered the woods
with the white anemonie which the children call Ladysmocks*

John Clare holds up his orchises and celadines to Wisdom.
'Eat flowers then,' replies the Gypsy. 'Serve harebells to your children.
Save petals against their schooling. Whittle pens from a thistle-stem.
If you can afford bouquets then you cannot be going hungry.'
'Aye, brother,' gruffs Clare, 'you were saying that about poetry.
I gained all this for the low charge of a three miles' walk
with poems yet to be written on some botanising topic
picked up from sheltered places where these wild souls grow.'
'Eat words then. Some must murder their supper.' The Gypsy
folds across a fence into the wood and leaps through shadow.
Windflowers, Grandmother's nightcaps, or what the children,
mishearing, call wooden enemies, lift drooping heads and listen
to moonlit rumour from behind bared branches. Wisdom Smith
paces like a fox between the trees. He freezes. Sinks to earth.

King of Cormorants

*& pieces of naked water such as ponds lakes & pools without fish
make me melancholly to look over it*

Then a jay jeers from the sobbing blossoms:
> *I always see a bit of home*
> *in every likely thing –*
> *a white-thorn hedge*
> *or bramble bush*
> *or pollard willow tree*
> *brings me my own homestead*
> *and the budding of the spring.*
A shrike stops her ear to her spiked tenants:
> *To be alive! To be alive!* Lord, how they sing.
Wild rains roam and rush around the Gypsy's tent.
Wisdom clears his throat and frowns over to his friend.
Mad Clare, 'poor John', wafts his coat over the campfire;
nay, over the whetted world. 'I am king,' he cries, 'of cormorants.'

The Friend of All Friends

Returned home out of Essex... and was soon at Northborough
but Mary was not there neither could I get any information about
her further than the old story of her being dead six years ago

'I walked the hard road home with my garrison, Wisdom.
I had my invisible army about me, all of us hungering.
I gained Northborough. My second wife Patty was home.
My true love Mary, they say she is dead. This was our ring.'
John Clare unclenches his palm. The Gypsy reaches, lightly,
and pretends to marvel. 'It is a fine craftily matter, John.
Our blacksmiths would wonder. To smelt the purity
of air, and hammer it to something hidden yet lovely.
You must have loved her, friend, as if she was your own.'
Wisdom Smith glances: 'What do you want for the thing?'
'I want Mary to live so I can believe the world alive again.'
'Patty is your wife.' But Dead Mary watches the Gypsy.
She stares out from John to his friend of all friends.
Believe in me, she whispers as John Clare breathes: 'Believe me.'

Harebells

& the little heath bell or harvest bell quakes to the wind
under the quick banks & warm furze...

John Clare puts down his violin. 'Is there quickening wisdom
in the road and heath that sits hushed in a home and family?
— I mean the music of life moving. Swallows, swans, fieldfares.
These are ever nearer to me, more so because they never stay.'
Wisdom Smith tugs corks on two bottles. He pulls a long face.
'John, I know no man more half-in or half-out of your race.
You covet our roving — you are no bad scraper at the fiddle —
but you will never join us because you love' — gestures Wisdom —
'you love all this. We are like the harebells around us, brother:
everywhere and unseen; clear-eyed as those night-blue bells;
rebounding from the trudge and trample of night and day;
outstaring weather; blooming on into the first autumn gales.'
The dusk wind blows out the lamps of all the heath's flowers.
'We die if we do not move, whereas John — John, you would die.'

The Strayed

My hopeless nerves are all unstrung

'The world plays me like a kite, Wisdom; fame
like a gale hauls me high, firm on my frame –
sunshine on a harvest will do the same;
but one bleak word, or no word, and the strain
wrenches all my string.' 'You live by the smile
and frown of men. You bind yourself servile
to the sobbings of sparrows. Forgo them.'
John Clare watches his children play on the green.
'I cannot leave Northborough, my wives and home.'
'Their doors will always be on a latch, John,
however far you choose to stray from them.
Look. At me. How often have I upped and gone
yet you see me as though I never strayed?
The world will leave you, brother. I shall stay.'

The Act

A chorredo has burreder peas than a Romany Chal.

Wisdom swings to his feet as if pulled by an invisible hand.
'I shall show how this world wags without making one sound.'
And the Gypsy transforms himself first into a lawyer. He bends
a burning eye on invisible jurors. He simpers. He stands on his head
as the Judge and thunders silent sentence. Then Wisdom levitates
to tip-toe in pity and pride as a Reverend bent over his Bible
while an invisible scaffold gasps and bounces from a rope's recoil.
The Gypsy hangs kicking until hacked down by invisible blades.
The world grinds to a stop on invisible springs, bearings and axis.
'Do you ever tell lies, Wisdom?' 'All the long day through, brother,'
laughs the Gypsy. He lights his long pipe beneath his hat's brim.
'But the brassest of lies' – the Gypsy plucks – 'are like this heather:
a charm against visible harm and' – he crushes it – 'invisible harm.'
And the friends look at each other across the invisible stage of grass.

The Gypsy and the Poet

far hid from the world's eye:
I fain would have some friend to wander nigh
– John Clare

My house moves nowhere, hauled by invisible horses.
Shades shift around me, warming their hands at my hearth.
It has rained speech-marks down the windows' pages,
gathering a broken language in pools on their ledges
before letting it slither into the hollows of the earth.
My child stares out of windows on a pouring planet.
To him perhaps it is raining everywhere and forever.
I told myself this once. It is why I do not forget it;
although forty years have passed yet I am no older.
When Gypsy people speak aloud to one another
across greenway and hollow-way they say sister and brother.
When mother or father speak aloud to their children
they say our own daughter and they say our own son.
I call out to my child, and he is everywhere, and she is everyone.

'Broken language': *Poggadi Jibb* or Romani

Notes

The Romani epigraphs to the Wisdom Smith sonnets are from *The Book of Wisdom of the Egyptians* and traditional Traveller songs. I do not offer a translation; meaning may be found within the poems. The English epigraphs are from John Clare's notebooks and poems.

'On Not Rushing at Waterfalls'
In the 1930s, the Chinese artist Chiang Yee visited and painted the Posforth Gill waterfalls in the Valley of Desolation above Bolton Abbey, the visit recorded in *The Silent Traveller in the Yorkshire Dales* (1940). The poem is a calligramme adaptation of his account of the visit.

The walking poems: these poems are written in forms taken from the natural world: calligrammes that mimic natural movement and natural sound. All these poems were also written on foot in Strid Wood in North Yorkshire and in the River Wharfe that spools through that wood. The poems were part of a Slow Art Trail commissioned by Chrysalis Arts sited within Strid Wood and were released as poetry films on iTunes U and YouTube.

'Pipping'
I painted most of these poems on species-specific bird boxes to create 'bard boxes'. The bard boxes were left to weather and then fixed to trees. Birds nested in a poem about themselves and their fledglings emerged from within the poem. The epigraphs are phonetic descriptions of bird-calls from the *Collins Bird Guide*.

'Fight'
After Federico García Lorca's 'Reyerta' from *Gypsy Ballads*.

'Foxes, Swans, Starlings'
Adapted from 'The Aurora Borealis' by Pål Brekke, *Scandinavian Review*, 17.